Lessons from a Border Collie Series

Written & Illustrated by Kriste Sveen

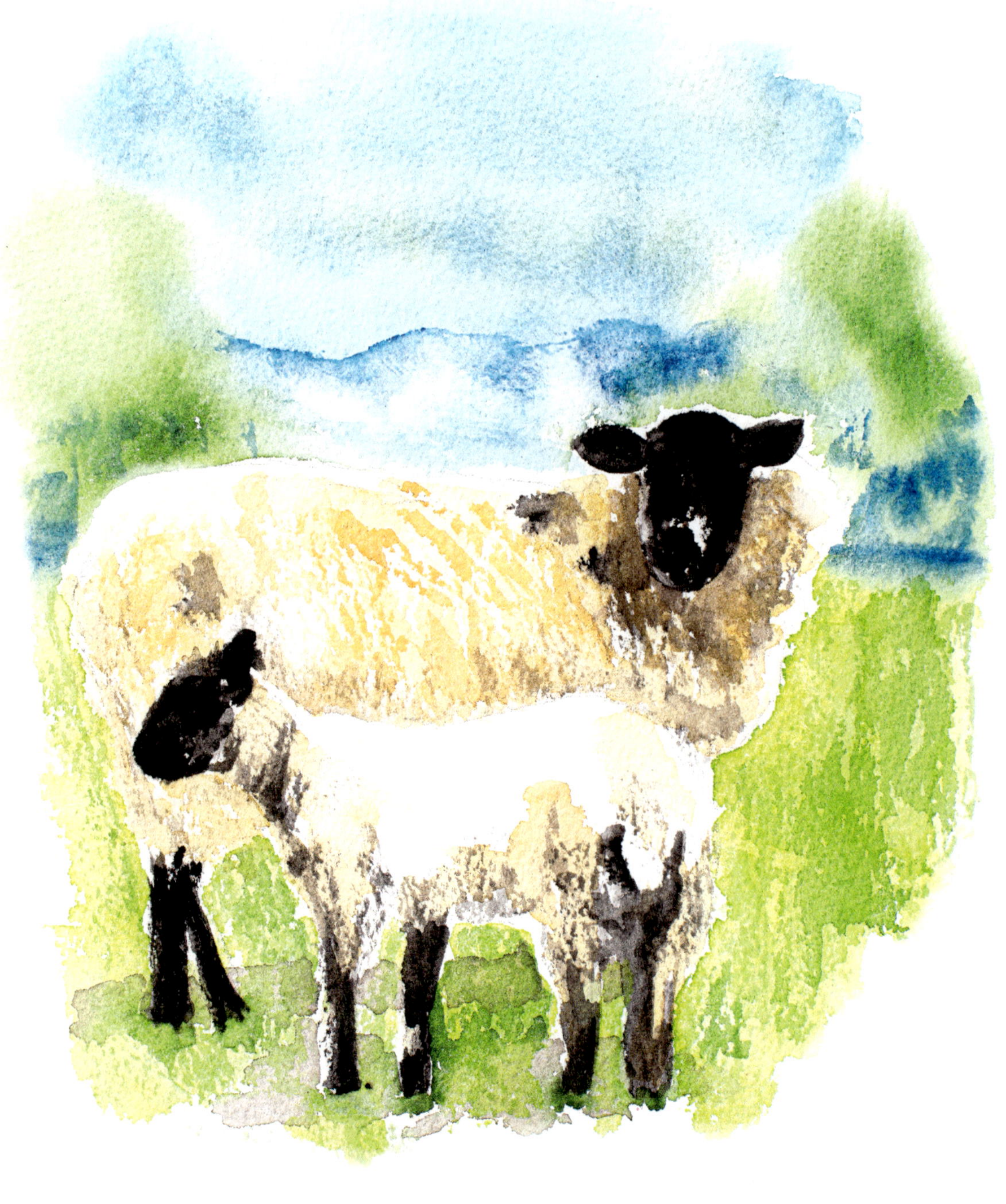

Introduction to Ike And The Shepherd of Psalm 23

Ike is a Border Collie and the third Border Collie that our family has raised over 28 years. We love all of the characteristics of the breed, especially when watching highly trained Border Collies work with sheep. Border Collies are often used by shepherds because they have qualities, when trained, that can help the shepherds with the sheep. When I began to train Ike, I noticed that these were some of the same qualities that I was teaching children about worshiping God together. In our adventures together, there were similarities of Ike as the sheep and me as his shepherd.

In my first book, **I Like Ike,** children learn how to approach God, with trust, belonging, joy, and humility. In **A Hike With Ike**, children learn what God is like through the creation that he has made. In **Ike And The Shepherd**, children learn about God in a deep and personal way through the metaphor of Psalm 23 and God as the Good Shepherd.

Here, I broke down Psalm 23 into nine sections, each with a story about Ike and the *Good Shepherd*. The stories about Ike show characteristics of sheep. But more importantly, each section describes a quality of God, *the Good Shepherd*, and provides the Hebrew name for that quality. With us as the sheep and God as the *Good Shepherd*, Psalm 23 helps us discover that we are frail humans who have many needs that the *Good Shepherd* can meet. In Psalm 23, we have two perspectives; what the sheep are like and what they need, and what God is like and what He does for us.

My hope is to help children discover how much God loves them. Jesus identified himself as the *Good Shepherd* in the Gospel of John, and used the same metaphor to illustrate things about himself and about us. He also connects Psalm 23 from the Old Testament with Himself, as God, the *Good Shepherd*.

In **Ike And The Shepherd**, we learn what the *Good Shepherd* is like, why we need him and how we can call on him by name. The Hebrew name of Jehovah is translated, "The God who is, who was and is to be". This is a very personal term for God and implies that we can be close to Him. Each descriptive name comes after Jehovah and gives another facet of God's character. Nine of God's names are hidden within Psalm 23. Calling God by name helps us get to know Him.

May we all see ourselves as sheep of the *Good Shepherd,* listening for his voice, following Him into restful green pastures, and allowing him to guide us along the right paths.

The Lord is my Shepherd.
Psalm 23:1

You can find sheep in many places in the world, some with rolling hills, green pastures and mountain trails. If you look long enough, you will also see their shepherd because sheep need someone to take care of them. Shepherds often have dogs to help them gather their sheep. In many places, shepherds use Border Collies like Ike, because Border Collies are smart, they listen and obey the shepherd's directions.

Ike is my Border Collie and I am his shepherd, who takes care of him. Since he was a puppy, I have fed him, cared for him, and taught him to listen to me. Ike knows my voice because we have spent a lot of time talking together. He trusts me to do good things for him. He hears me from far away and recognizes the sound of my voice. He even knows the sound of my footsteps and gets excited when I come home. When he was little, I called him by his name and then hugged and pet him when he came to me. He began to learn that by coming to me he would be comforted.

In this picture, the shepherd is calling the sheep by their names and they come running. They must have spent a lot of time together, because they know the sound of his voice. He speaks with a gentle voice, which calms the sheep and keeps them from getting scared. Once they know the shepherd's voice, they won't listen to a stranger.

Do you know that not only sheep have shepherds? You and I each have a shepherd that knows our names and knows everything about us. God is our shepherd and we will call him the *Good Shepherd*. I have started to recognize the *Good Shepherd's* voice in my thoughts as I've spent more and more time listening to him and trusting him to take care of me.

I wonder if you know about this Shepherd.

Let's follow along and see what we can learn from the Good Shepherd and the sheep.

"The shepherd calls his own sheep by name and leads them out. When he gets them all out, he leads them and they follow because they are familiar with his voice. They won't follow a stranger's voice but will scatter because they aren't used to the sound of it."

HEBREW NAME FOR GOD

Jehovah- Rohi [Raah]
The Lord is My Shepherd

I have all that I need.
Psalm 23:1B

Ike is an anxious dog. He worries about things that are moving and not in his control. If I get ahead of him, he barks and is worried that I am not near him. When I am near him, I can calm him down and he becomes content just because I am there. He might *want* to be in control, but I know that he *needs* me to be in control in order for him to relax.

It looks like we started following the shepherd at the end of the day, but the shepherd's work is not done, even when the sheep sleep. We come to a pen with four walls. This is called a sheepfold. It could be made with wood or stones, like this one. It is a place to keep the sheep safe at night. The shepherd guides the sheep into the sheepfold. It has an opening to let the sheep in and out, and the shepherd is the gate. He lies down at the door to protect the sheep. It looks like Ike is going to lie down next to the shepherd for the night.

Just like the sheep relax and are content when they are near the shepherd, I feel the most relaxed when I remember that the *Good Shepherd* is always near me and will never leave me. I can tell him about all of my worries and anxieties and he will know what I need. He knows everything about me. I am trying to be content with whatever happens to me because I know that the *Good Shepherd* is near me and will take care of me. I need to let him be in control. The more time that I spend with the *Good Shepherd*, I see that he is the provider of all the good things that I have ever received.

I wonder if you can think of things the Good Shepherd has provided for you.

I wonder if you could tell your worries or anxieties to the Good Shepherd.

I wonder if you can tell the difference between things that you may want and things that you need.

"The one who enters through the gate is the shepherd of the sheep. The gatekeeper opens the gate for him and the sheep recognize his voice and come to him. Yes, I am the gate. Those who come in through me will be saved." *John 10:2-3,9 NLT*

HEBREW NAME FOR GOD
Jehovah-Jireh
The Lord is My Provider

He lets me rest in green meadows;
He leads me beside peaceful streams.
Psalm 23:2

Ike loves to take walks and play fetch with the ball. He needs lots of exercise. He would play fetch all day if he could, even when he is tired, he keeps bringing the ball back and putting it in my lap. After a while, I need to take the ball away and tell him to lie down so that he will rest.

Sometimes, the shepherd needs to lead the sheep a long way to find fresh grass to eat and calm water to drink. Sheep won't drink from water that is moving. They get scared. They will only drink from water that is calm and peaceful. It looks like the sheep are about to take a drink. Does this look like peaceful water?

The shepherd watches the sheep to see when they are tired. They have been walking and eating a long time, and this looks like a good place to rest. Sheep won't choose to rest on their own, they would keep wandering and eating. The shepherd calms the sheep by singing or playing a flute so that they begin to relax. When they hear the music, they begin to feel calm and safe. Then the sheep begin to lie down and rest.

When there is peacefulness all around, it is called "Shalom" or "All as it should be." Sometimes we need to be told to take a rest. Just as I need to tell Ike to lie down and stop working, sometimes the *Good Shepherd* tells me to take a rest by the things that happen to me. He knows that we need rest from busy days. The *Good Shepherd* will watch over us as we rest, because he never tires. If we follow the *Good Shepherd*, he will show us when and where to rest and feel his peace.

I wonder if you like to listen to a song before you go to sleep.

I wonder what peacefulness feels like to you.

"Yes, I am the gate. Those who come in through me will be saved. They will come and go freely and will find good pastures." *John 10:9 NLT*

HEBREW NAME FOR GOD

Jehovah-Shalom
The Lord is Our Peace

He renews my strength.
Psalm 23:3

When Ike plays fetch, he tries so hard to catch the ball that sometimes he goes too fast and hurts his muscles by catching it in an awkward position. I notice if he is limping or has a hurt paw. If he has any cuts or scrapes, I clean them and make him rest until they heal. We don't play ball until he heals and is strong again.

In the same way, throughout the day the shepherd inspects and watches the sheep to see if any sheep are limping or weak. He looks to see if they have any wounds or scratches. Sheep can get very dirty because their wool is covered in lanolin and dirt sticks to it. The only way they will get clean is if their shepherd cleans them. If he is a good shepherd, he will sometimes use an oil to loosen the dirt, smooth out the tangles in their wool and disinfect their scratches. The oil is a balm that can heal cuts from thorns or dry skin from rubbing against branches. If the sheep are sick, the shepherd gives them medicine so they can become strong again. He knows them so well that he sees everything that they might need.

Sometimes, medicine and ointment can only do so much, and I need to ask the *Good Shepherd* to do the rest of the healing. Not only can he heal the wounds of our body, but the *Good Shepherd* also heals the wounds of our hearts. He is the only one who knows how we were made and what needs to be healed for us to feel better.

I wonder if you can remember a time that you did not feel well.

I wonder if you have ever asked the Good Shepherd to heal you and make you feel better.

"I will give you back your health and heal your wounds." *Jeremiah 30:17 NIV*
"He heals the brokenhearted and bandages their wounds." *Psalm 147:3 NLT*

HEBREW NAME FOR GOD

Jehovah-Rophe [Rapha]
The Lord Who Heals

He guides me along right paths,
Bringing honor to his name.
Psalm 23:3b

Ike is a herding dog, which means he naturally runs side to side behind me or children, to get them to move forward down a path. Sometimes he grabs the edge of my robe to get me to move toward the door to take him for a walk. He is always ready for a walk but before we go, he looks up at me to see which way he should go.

After their rest, the shepherd gets the sheep moving again. Unlike Ike, sheep would stay in the same place and eat the grass down to the roots, until there would be nothing left. While sheep are busy eating, they don't pay attention to where they are or where the rest of the flock has gone. They can get lost and separated from the flock very easily. They will then walk in endless circles, very confused because they have no sense of direction. They need a shepherd to guide them where to go, whose voice they know, or they will refuse to move. Herding dogs can help the shepherd from the back and the sides, to encourage the sheep to move towards the shepherd. The shepherd leads the way because he is the only one who knows the right way to go.

Ike always looks to me to know which way to turn. He wants to know what to do next. In the same way, I ask the *Good Shepherd* which way I should go when I am confused. He knows our names and knows just the right path for each of us so that we don't just keep eating roots. We can choose to go our own way or follow his way in the right paths that will give him honor and give us abundant life.

I wonder if you have ever been lost and didn't know which way to go.

What did it feel like to be lost?

"You were lost sheep with no idea who you were or where you were going. Now you're named and kept for good by the Shepherd of your souls." *1Peter 2:25 MSG*

HEBREW NAME FOR GOD

Jehovah-Tsidkenu
The Lord is Our Righteousness

Even when I walk through the darkest valley, I will not be afraid.
Psalm 23:4

Once when Ike and I were in our backyard next to the woods, I attached his leash to a chair. Often, deer walk through our backyard and this time they came very close to us. I tried to scare them away, but it scared Ike and he took off chasing them, chair, leash and all. I ran after him as fast as I could but couldn't catch up and didn't know which way Ike had gone. I was so afraid that I would never find him and that he was lost forever. After a long time of walking, calling Ike's name, I turned around to see Ike trotting up behind me. He must have gotten stuck on a tree, because he had lost his leash, collar and chair. However, Ike must have heard my voice and found me.

Sheep wander off and can't find their way back to the flock. The shepherd counts his sheep and can tell when one of them is missing. He hurriedly leaves the flock and goes out after the lost one. The sheep can be scared all alone and not know what to do. Sheep can fall into holes, get hurt and can't get up. The shepherd must go quickly and find the lost one and carry it back to the flock.

I am always watchful of Ike so that he doesn't run away and get lost, but sometimes I slip up. It is reassuring to me that the *Good Shepherd* keeps a watchful eye on me, one of *his* sheep, and he will never lose me wherever I wander. Whatever dark place we might find ourselves in, nothing can keep the *Good Shepherd's* love from finding us. We do not need to be afraid, for he will always find us if we call.

I wonder if you have ever been afraid.

What made you feel afraid?

"I give them eternal life, and they will never perish. No one can snatch them away from me, for my Father has given them to me, and he is more powerful than anyone else. No one can snatch them from the Father's hand. The Father and I are one."
John 10:28-30 NLT

HEBREW NAME FOR GOD

Jehovah-Sabaoth
The Lord is My Defender, My Stronghold - Lord of Hosts

For you are close beside me.
Psalm 23:4b

Where we live, there are coyotes who prowl around at night looking for food. If they are hungry enough, they have been known to stalk large dogs. We sometimes see them during the day on our walks. Ike might growl at them, but he sticks close to my side. I am careful not to leave Ike alone outside at night, or even in the daylight. I am always near him when he is outside.

Since Ike and I have been following the shepherd, the shepherd has not left the sheep alone. He is always taking care of them by guiding them, healing them, feeding them, comforting them, or protecting them from wolves. A good shepherd will always stand between the sheep and danger, where an ordinary shepherd might run away and leave the sheep alone.

I am so glad that the *Good Shepherd* would never run away or leave me alone. It makes me feel safe knowing that the *Good Shepherd* is always with me and close beside me.

I wonder if you have ever felt alone.

I wonder if you feel safe knowing that the Good Shepherd is always close beside you, even if you can't see him.

"I am the Good Shepherd. The Good Shepherd sacrifices his life for the sheep. A hired hand will run when he sees a wolf coming. He will abandon the sheep because they don't belong to him and he isn't their shepherd. And so the wolf attacks them and scatters the flock. The hired hand runs away because he's working only for the money and doesn't really care about the sheep. I am the Good Shepherd. I know my own sheep, and they know me, just as my Father knows me and I know the Father. So I sacrifice my life for the sheep." *John 10:11-15 NLT*

HEBREW NAME FOR GOD

Jehovah-Shammah
The Lord is There, the Lord is With Me.

Your rod and your staff protect and comfort me.
You prepare a feast for me in the presence of my enemies.
Psalm 23:4c,5

As I said before, Ike is an anxious dog, and wants to be in control, but he doesn't know which way to go. He needs me to act as a shepherd to guide him. Sometimes, he picks up a stick and carries it in his mouth the entire walk. It seems to calm and comfort him. I use a leash when we walk, to guide him in the way he should go, and to protect him from running off and getting into trouble.

In the same way, the shepherd's staff seems to calm the sheep. It comforts them when the shepherd uses it to touch them gently as they go along, letting them know he is near or to guide them along the right path. Sometimes the sheep even use it to scratch themselves by rubbing up against it. The shepherd holds it high like a banner so the sheep can see it and know that they belong to him. He uses it to pull sheep out of thorn bushes when they get stuck, or rescue them when they fall into creeks. The shepherd also carries a rod to protect the sheep from snakes, coyotes or wolves. While they feast on high mountain tablelands or mesas of rich grasses, the shepherd is on guard with his staff and rod to protect the sheep against all the animals that could harm them.

Just as Ike's leash and stick protect him and comfort him, the shepherd's rod protects the sheep and his staff comforts them. It reminds me of how the *Good Shepherd* protects me and helps me stay on the right path. Because Ike belongs to me and I want to take good care of him, I want him to feast on good food. Because I belong to the *Good Shepherd,* he wants to take good care of me because he loves me. He will lead me to places like high pastures that are spacious and rich in food for my soul so I can feast unafraid.

I wonder if you have been to a big feast with lots of food.

I wonder if there were people there who loved you and cared about you. Can you remember how it made you feel?

I wonder what food is good for your soul.

"They will come and go freely and will find good pastures. The thief's purpose is to steal and kill and destroy. My purpose is to give them a rich and satisfying life."
John 10:9,10 NLT

HEBREW NAME FOR GOD

Jehovah-Nissi
The Lord is my Banner, and My Protector

You honor me by anointing my head with oil.
My cup overflows with blessings.
Surely your goodness and unfailing love will pursue me
All the days of my life and I will live in the house of the Lord forever.
Psalm 23:5-6

When Ike came home to live with us, one of the first things I did was to get him his own collar. It showed the world that he was now part of our flock, and that we would take care of him and give him love and good things. Even though some days he does everything we want him to do, there are other days that he messes up. No matter what, I will continue to love him and want to do good things for him every day.

This is a picture of a beautiful summer day. The sun is warm and the grass is still cool up in the mountains. The temperature is perfect, not too hot, and not too cool, with a bit of a breeze blowing. Even in these perfect, beautiful conditions, the shepherd still has work to do with his sheep. In these lush pastures, bugs and flies start to irritate the sheep. The shepherd goes to each sheep and gently puts oil on their heads and noses to seal their skin so the flies won't bite them. Ike can also be bothered by flies and ticks, so I put a special oil on his coat to keep them away.

Just as the shepherd uses oil on all of his own sheep, sometimes we use oil to anoint our heads as a symbol that we are part of the *Good Shepherd's* flock and set apart for Him. Just as the oil sets the sheep apart from flies, we can know that we are set apart and belong to the *Good Shepherd*. Even when we mess up, he still pursues us with goodness and unfailing love all the days of our lives and we can someday live with Him forever.

I wonder if you can imagine a place of love and beauty and goodness.

I wonder what it would look like, sound like, feel like and smell like.

"My sheep listen to my voice; I know them, and they follow me. I give them eternal life, and they will never perish. *John 10:27,28 NLT*

HEBREW NAME FOR GOD

Jehovah-M'Kaddesh
The Lord is my Sanctifier - sets me apart as his

Psalm 23

The Lord is my shepherd;

I have all that I need.

He lets me rest in green meadows; he leads me beside peaceful streams.

He renews my strength.

He guides me along right paths, bringing honor to his name.

Even when I walk through the darkest valley, I will not be afraid,

for you are close beside me.

Your rod and your staff protect and comfort me.

You prepare a feast for me in the presence of my enemies.

You honor me by anointing my head with oil.

My cup overflows with blessings.

Surely your goodness and unfailing love will pursue me all the days of my life,

and I will live in the house of the Lord forever.

Psalms 23:1-6
New Living Translation

HEBREW NAMES OF GOD

Jehovah-Rohi [Raah]
The Lord is My Shepherd

Jehovah-Jireh
The Lord is My Provider

Jehovah-Shalom
The Lord is Our Peace

Jehovah-Rophe [Rapha]
The Lord Who Heals

Jehovah-Tsidkenu
The Lord is Our Righteousness

Jehovah-Sabaoth
The Lord is My Defender, My Stronghold

Jehovah-Shammah
The Lord is There, The Lord is with Me

Jehovah-Nissi
The Lord is My Banner, and My Protector

Jehovah-M'Kaddesh
The Lord is My Sanctifier

ABOUT THE AUTHOR

Kriste Sveen studies worship, practices worship arts, and teaches children how to worship. She is an artist that enjoys encouraging others to use art in order to hear God and live a more creative life. Ike is her third Border Collie that she and her husband have raised, along with five children. She is the proud grandparent of three beautiful grandchildren. Kriste, her husband David, and Ike, split their time between Wheaton, IL, Sawyer, MI, and Beaver Creek, CO.

Kriste can be reached for workshops and speaking engagements at:
kriste.inspiredcreations@gmail.com
www.inspiredcreations.org
www.themakersspace.us

Acknowledgments

The Young Children and Worship book by **Sonja Stewart** has influenced
and guided me in teaching children about worship.
Her Montessori based method helps children enter into story
and wonder about God.

I would like to acknowledge the teachings of **Scottie May**, Ph.D.
Wheaton College and her students. They taught the method of Sonja Stewart
and wrote a nine week curriculum for children based on The Good Shepherd.
I started writing from that foundation.

I would also like to acknowledge the teaching of **Vivien Hibbert**,
who first showed me the nine hidden names of God in Psalm 23.
I have continued teaching the uncountable names of God to children,
in order to show them God's expansiveness
and the many facets of His character.

Vivien Hibbert Ministries and The Heart of Worship Blog.
http://theheartoftheworshiper.blogspot.com/2013/02/the-names-of-god.html
http://theheartoftheworshiper.blogspot.com/search?q=Jehovah

Ike And The Shepherd - Lessons from a Border Collie

Copyright © 2023 Kriste Sveen ISBN 978-1-7347988-4-5

Scripture quotations marked [MSG} are taken from the Message,
copyright © 1993, 2002, 2018 by Eugene H. Peterson.
Used by permission of NavPress. All rights reserved. Represented by Tyndall House Publishers.

Scripture quotations marked [NLT] are taken from the Holy Bible, New Living Translation,
copyright © 1996, 2004, 2015, by Tyndale House Foundation.
Used by permission of Tyndale House Publishers, Carol Stream, Illinois 60188.

All rights reserved.

Made in the USA
Monee, IL
18 September 2024